The Cathedral Is Burning

A Lamentation

poems by

Betsy Orient Bernfeld

Finishing Line Press
Georgetown, Kentucky

The Cathedral Is Burning

A Lamentation

for my mother and grandmothers

Copyright © 2021 by Betsy Orient Bernfeld
ISBN 978-1-64662-554-3 First Edition
All rights reserved under International and Pan-American Copyright Conventions. No part of this book may be reproduced in any manner whatsoever without written permission from the publisher, except in the case of brief quotations embodied in critical articles and reviews.

Publisher: Leah Huete de Maines

Editor: Christen Kincaid

Cover Photo: Betsy Bernfeld

Author Photo: Andrea Leoncavallo

Cover Design: Elizabeth Maines McCleavy

Order online: www.finishinglinepress.com
also available on amazon.com

Author inquiries and mail orders:
Finishing Line Press
P. O. Box 1626
Georgetown, Kentucky 40324
U. S. A.

Table of Contents

The Cathedral is Burning 1

Alamo Wash 16

Cathedral 18

If I Were Going to Build a House 20

The Woman and the Coyote 21

Trespass at 820 East Grant 24

Seeing the Light 27

Great Great Great Grandmothers 30

George Washington Burning 35

Walk a Mile in my Shoes 36

Breathless Awe 37

As Spring Unfurls During the Pandemic 38

The Gulbransen 41

Candle once laid 43

In the Forest of Unknown Trees 45

A Sip from the Claret Cup 48

At Rachel's Well 50

A Hebrew Lamenation 52

Zero Percent Contained 55

Mother in the City of God 57

Walking through the Mercy Door at Sacred Heart Chapel on Summer Solstice under Strawberry Moon 59

"The Mothers: Las Madres Project. No Mas Lágrimas"
created by Valarie Lee James
with Antonia Gallegos, Deborah McCullough and Cesar Lopez.
Photo by Betsy Bernfeld.

The Cathedral Is Burning

I.

On Monday, April 15, 2019
around 7:00 p.m. local time
at the very start of Holy Week
in the very heart of Paris
the cathedral burned.
Notre-Dame de Paris,
Our Lady of Paris.

Flames were seen through the rose windows
and the spire collapsed through the roof
the city just stopped
the people remembered
their long unused prayers
and sang *Ave Maria*
in the street.

Ted DeGrazia's "Mission in the Sun"
Photo by Betsy Bernfeld.

On Monday, May 30, 2017
around 6:00 p.m. local time
Memorial Day weekend
in the foothills above Tucson
the chapel burned.
The Mission in the Sun
of Our Lady of Guadalupe,
Our Lady as native to Tucson soil
as the desert sand.

Neighbors reported the smoke
and within three minutes
rural fire fighters doused the flames
but the roof was gone
adobe walls saturated
frescoes melted to the floor
the altar painting of Guadalupe
reduced to black residue.

Benedictine Monastery, Tucson, Arizona
Photo by Betsy Bernfeld.

On Monday, February 26, 2018
after vespers after the sun
reached the horizon
the building's carved stone façade
reflecting the purple of sunset
the turquoise dome
capturing the last light of day
the Tucson Benedictine monastery
of the Sisters of Perpetual Adoration
was sold closed and locked.

"Bighorn Fire," Santa Catalina Mountains
Photo by Paul Ingram/TucsonSentinel.com.

During the day above Tucson
smoke billowed off Cathedral Peak
the federal climate report concluding
more heat and drought
less water bigger wildfires
fewer native trees.
During the night
the fire was a red wound
growing on the mountaintop.

"The Mothers: *Las Madres Project. No Mas Lágrimas*"
created by Valarie Lee James
with Antonia Gallegos, Deborah McCullough and Cesar Lopez.
Photo by Betsy Bernfeld.

Since the year 2000
some 3,000 refugees
temples of the Holy Spirit
from Mexico and Central America
were found sun-burned dead on the desert
near Ajo, Arizona.

II.

Notre-Dame's foundation stone was laid in 1163 by Pope Alexander III, the cathedral completed 107 years later. "The history is ours. And it burns." *(President Emmanuel Marcon)*

Artist Ted DeGrazia bought 10 acres in the Santa Catalina foothills above Tucson in 1949. In the Spanish tradition, he first built a little mission in memory of Padre Eusebio Kino, dedicated to Our Lady of Guadalupe. "A place in which to begin to believe." *(Ted DeGrazia)*

In 1935 Bishop Daniel J. Gercke invited the Benedictine Sisters of Perpetual Adoration to build a monastery in Tucson. The Sisters laid their cornerstone, quarried from the nearby Santa Rita Mountains, and opened the monastery in 1940. *"Viva Christo Rey!"* (the Sisters' dedication)

"I have come to set the earth on fire, and how I wish it were already blazing!" *(Jesus, Lk 12:49)*

> The history is ours and it burns
> to begin to believe
> Viva!
> Blazing!

III.

The Cathedral's main bell Emanuelle
and twin bell towers survived.
The rose windows
the Great Organ
the Crown of Thorns
splinters of the True Cross
and one of the Holy Nails
saved.
The copper rooster from the top of the fallen spire
with relics for the protection of Paris
intact.
"Paris without *Notre-Dame*, madness."

Among the charred remains
of the Mission in the Sun
were crosses of various sizes
melted picture frames
cherubs and small statues
chips of glass
"a place for remembering."

The mortuary workers
loaded my father's body
into their station wagon
but I knew he didn't want to go.
I invited his spirit into my car instead
and we headed up Swan Road to DeGrazia's
as fast as he wanted
really really fast
"it will never be the same."

In the sanctuary
in a canopy above the altar

of the Sisters of Perpetual Adoration
is still poised
a Pelican in her Piety.

In time of famine in ancient belief
a pelican mother would pierce
her own breast with pointed beak
and feed her young her own blood.
In ancient art a pelican mother
with piercéd heart a sacred symbol
a feminine emblem
of sacrificing self.

Charity gold-leafed
prayer white-feathered
wounds red-lipped neck curled
beak at rest on breast
Sisters gone extinct.

In 120-degree temperature days without rain
a body within a few hours
has a rock-hard nose earlobes and fingertips.
Within a few days all moisture is gone
wicked into the desert sand
a chalky outline all that remains.

The fires were started by renovation, burning votive candles, lost vocations, avid development, immigration policies,

    history burning belief blazing madness.

IV.

On April 16, 2018
at 6:00 p.m. local time
at Notre Dame campus in Indiana
the bells of the Basilica of the Sacred Heart
tolled 50 times
for the 50 Hail Marys of Our Lady's Rosary
marking the beginning of rebuilding
Notre-Dame de Paris.

In May 2019
above the Mission altar
caretakers reinstated DeGrazia's
early beeswax painting
of Our Lady of Guadalupe
the chapel open to the sky
door closed until further notice
guarded by a giant prickly pear
beautifully purpled by the cold winter
getting ready to bloom.

On June 11, 2019
after three days of deliberation
after 88 more migrant deaths
the felony case against Scott Warren
for assisting two refugees in Ajo
was dismissed due to a hung jury.

In October 2018, while awaiting construction cranes, the Benedictine Monastery of the Sisters of Perpetual Adoration was opened as a temporary sanctuary for asylum-seekers from Central America. During the next ten months, about 13,000 refugees passed through its doors aided by about 500 Tucson volunteers. The activities director encouraged the frightened children to "draw something that you love."

"What is that orange triangle with red flames?"
"Es mi madre."
　It is my mother.

Editor's Update:

At his retrial in November 2019, Scott Warren was acquitted.

DeGrazia's Mission in the Sun was rededicated in December 2019.

Luxury apartments were developed at the site of Tucson's Benedictine Monastery—34 apartments within the monastery itself and 255 apartments surrounding it.

In June 2020, a lightning-caused fire swept the Santa Catalina Mountains north of Tucson, encompassing about 119,000 acres over a six-week period. Finally the monsoon put it out.

Reconstruction of *Notre-Dame de Paris* was delayed due to the coronavirus.

"Marble Waters" created by Robin Riley.
Photo by Betsy Bernfeld

Alamo Wash

now dry
flows into the Rillito River
now dry
flows into the Santa Cruz River
now mostly dry
once running year-round
flows into the Gila River
now mostly dry
once running year-round
flows into the mighty Colorado River
largely depleted
when it reaches Arizona
totally depleted
by the time it reaches the Pacific.

I drop into Alamo Wash
sliding down a steep hill of packed dirt
made slippery by a sprinkling of coarse sand
with the dog
but today the dog doesn't even want to go
too hot too dry
trees hanging with crinkled pods of abandoned beans
a surprise of one yellow flower
what is it that I am seeking daily
as I slip down plunge down skid down screech down
into Alamo Wash
now dry.

Where Alamo Wash
flows into the Rillito River
now dry
there is a bridge above me
decorated with a mosaic "Marble Waters"
each exquisite water droplet portrayed
in a unique cluster of colorful tiles
each ornament a universe
blue muddied with orange disks

tiny red and gold puries eyes
that see it all see too much
flowing toward the Santa Cruz
now mostly dry.

I drop down
even at night
as I close my eyes
into Alamo Wash
I skip down scrape down leap down dream down
those first few steps
into the secret flow of solitude
threading through
without water
as far as the ocean.

Cathedral

Immaculate Conception Cathedral in Kansas City, Missouri
was constructed in 1898, the same year
my grandmother was born in Wallace, Missouri.
The walls were astonishingly thick,
door jams a foot and a half deep. Her bones
were hard and thin, skin like yellowed
parchment stained purple with blood
from the IVs. This holy place.
I wonder how many times my grandmother
was here, head bowed in her Belgian lace
mantilla. The constant whoosh of oxygen.
The statues were lifelike and bloody,
St. Stephen stoned, the pews too short
for my knees. She was shrunken
under five feet tall, a white angel,
hands sculpted, each joint a round ball,
each digit slightly crooked from its neighbor.
Watching out the window, cars slowly circled
looking for a place to park. Someone abandoned
his car in the loading zone and dashed
for the hospital entrance. Golden tabernacle,
high airy ceiling, dark wood polished,
tiers of candles inside red glass flickering
with the prayers of the faithful.
One hundred years old. I want to die.
Why can't I die? Why won't you let me die?
Our Father who art in heaven, deliver us.
I filed her nails into perfect crescents,
buffing them until they shone.
Yellow orange sunset was blinding in the window.
Please, please let me die. Dark wood creaking,
thick velvet curtains on the confessional,
turquoise tube in her nose, brutally perfect breastbone
prominent on her chest, hands gnarled like a tree root.
"I am the root of all that," she said one Christmas Eve
as her children, grandchildren
and great grandchildren paraded past her,

"root" pronounced the Missouri way
like foot, Christ sitting waiting
in the cathedral.

If I Were Going to Build a House

I would not start with two stained glass windows
but it so happens that two stained glass windows
is what I have to start with. Windows
is not necessarily a bad start I mean
sunlight is already available
and what is the purpose of windows
but to stand between you and sky.

If I were going to build a house
I would not start with an oaken front door
sturdy and supportive as it might be
with a pre-installed doorbell even but a door
is what I have and night is already available
and what is the purpose of a door
but to stand as barrier between you and me
holding on by knob and hinge.

You laugh and say a house must start
with a foundation, a solid one at that,
and I say why? My stained glass windows
hold bunches of purple grapes and green leaves.
I'd say I have a regal start, a holy start. A house
is not just a foundation and a brick wall
but also doors and windows so that you can see
outside from inside so that you can get outside
from inside or inside from outside. At dawn
sunlight separates into slivers of gold and green.
At dusk my windows cast the purple light of wine.
You ring the bell and come in.

The Woman and the Coyote

The first thing she noticed was the animal's
luxurious coat, thick and healthy. She paused
on one side of Saratoga Street, coyote
on the other. She wore the same sweats
she had slept in just throwing on
her wind parka taking her mug
of hot very caffeinated tea heading
out the front door for a quiet walk
before husband and children awoke.
The two stood still and stared.

She was utterly immersed in domesticity
dirty dishes in the sink oatmeal for breakfast
dryer loads of clothes on the sofa
toys paints papers everywhere
musical instruments ballet shoes
princess dresses spilling out of cubbies
never a neat moment splatters on the stove
spots on the windows coats on the floor,
but who knows what a coyote is thinking.

After several morning encounters she realized
the coyote had made a home in a wide
passage between two houses on Saratoga
packed with trees tall grasses overgrown
rose bushes dandelions crowding
an indistinct trail. They met in the park
once, too, at twilight, the coyote
streaking past not low like a dog but high
and silent graceful as speeding light.

She knew not to step too close, imagine
too much, two creatures so wild so self-
abandoned they could harbor another's
heart rise at every cry for milk walk
danger in stride with joy lose liters
of blood stagger on between trees

through tangles of weeds gone to seed
on uncertain trails gentleness as deep-
seated as fury in protecting pups so which
is woman, which is coyote?

Photo by Betsy Bernfeld.

Trespass at 820 East Grant

I stole the front door
as soon as I knew the City
had condemned the property.
Oh I went through legal channels
as well you know the emails letters
and phone calls supposedly allowing
me access as former owner
all red tape bullshit of course
because when I showed up with
my sheath of paperwork and yellow
hardhat the scrawny young cousin
of the contractor with a self-important
clipboard in hand and a phone bud
in his ear threw me out.

When I stole the front door
it emboldened other vandals to slip in
to take the age-darkened pine paneling
and built-in bookshelves but lo
and behold they couldn't get the pine
paneling or bookshelves out so double
triple toenailed in by the young man
who installed them using hammer and handsaw
at night after work by the headlights
of his squeaky Chevy every nail
saying he loved her his wife
now pregnant with their third child
so they broke the windows in fury.

The City then was furious
with such an eyesore so close
to the road in their urban renewal
project and across the street
from Walmart parking which
was the reason for the decision
to tear down the house rather
than interfere with sales tax so they

put the screws to the contractor
who nagged the bulldozer operator
who still dinked around on the next-
door property unable to condone
the killing of the vintage cottage.

And so doorless the house
was last man standing in
the wrecked block all during
the Christmas holidays.
The walls weren't an easy takedown
either built first by the young man
who knew how to build walls but
not floors then he rushed the roof
afraid for the monsoon and indeed
it did hit but he napped securely
in the dirt of his would-be bedroom
and eventually poured the floors
through the front door opening
and finally he built the door.

The door was constructed from
two by six boards when two by
sixes were actually two by six
set vertically backed diagonally
by knotty pine shiplap
glued and nailed matured and
hardened by now with hand-wrought
iron hinges a tarnished round doorknob
and an old-fashioned ding dong doorbell
it weighed a ton as I well know.

On January 2 serious deconstruction
began the City brought in its
Tyrannosaurus Wrecker which stood
a full story above the house and
ate it from the roof down in big
bucket loads the debris dumped
in piles of metal glass brick wood

at night a swarm of takers invaded
like ants picking off everything
that could be sold for scrap or burned
the remnants now probably all over
the city and blue sky someone
even stole a chunk of the sidewalk.
It took the big tractor three full days
to level the tiny house—a budget
overrun—but there was little to take
to the dump afterwards they covered
the hole with a crapload of pale dirt.

The disembodied door leans
against the wall of my garage
still speaking to me with its
gruff voice: You are not
going to get in this door.
Keep out. Stay away.
Ding dong.
Father.

Seeing the Light

> *My eye has found the light, and the light*
> *itself has made me love the light.*
> *St. Catherine of Siena*

When a meteorite is coming, its bright
light flashing across the sky, traveling
millions of miles at thousands of feet
per second from an asteroid belt
or unknown celestial explosion,
full of hot exotic metals, a message
from heaven, unpredicted unexpected
angel fire, don't look at it,
duck and cover.

Such pieces of familial advice follow
me everywhere so that I am afraid
to look at the pale ivory crescent
moon without a gun in my hand.

It is a long drive to the sea, crossing
the glaring Southwest desert, I hardly dare
open my eyes even to write these words.
My mother warns that drug traffickers
drive this road at night at one hundred
with no headlights in the wrong lane.
My sister says don't use cruise control
in the rain, you could hydroplane and flip.
You exclaim that it's daylight and not raining.
The highway is lined with old mountain ranges,
rages, reduced to skeletons of themselves,
a few knobby teeth and pointy bones left,
voices once mighty and fiery. More eternal,
or less, comes the City of Los Angeles.

Were we not safer back at my mother's
house where people stole the air
conditioner off the roof and painted
graffiti on the patio wall?

I crawl out of the boat's frigid cabin
in my black winter jacket, black wool
ski cap, dark glasses, with coffee thick
from the French press and drop stiffly
to the blinding white cockpit locker where
you have wiped off the morning dew and
laid out our breakfast on a paper towel—
three hard boiled eggs, peeled and hovering
beside a salt shaker, a banana and a bear
claw. The morning breezes haven't stirred
in the marina and the foghorn of LA Lighthouse
persistently calls, "you're safe, you're safe."
You encourage me to take off my hat and sunglasses,
get a little sunshine on my face. I protest that the sun
is too bright, but I try it. Even with my eyelids
tightly clasped, the world is yellow, yellow,
yellow. I turn my head back and forth to escape
the light. Diagonal black lines shaft through
the glow and sparkles explode like wind
hitting the water.

I withstand the beauty
as long as I can, then clap my hands
over my face, but the dark is no longer
dark, it's impossibly rosy.

Mariah Chesnut Cox
Photo from the Collection of Phyllis A. Orient.

Great Great Great Grandmothers

My great great great grandmothers
were from Kentucky and Missouri,
two slave states,
but they were white,
freeborn.

Easter Chesnut, "née Evans," was born in 1782 in Todd, Kentucky during the Revolutionary War. She married Abraham Chesnut in 1801. Easter did not have the right to vote, and as soon as she married, she lost her right to own property. She started giving birth at age 20 and produced nine children thereafter, spaced one to three years apart, until she died in 1820 at age 38 as her last child was born.

Martha Chesnut   1802
Elizabeth Chesnut   1804
John Chesnut   1806
Evan Chesnut   1808
Patience Chesnut   1810
Polly Ann Chesnut   1813
Easter Chesnut   1815
Abraham Chesnut   1818
Andrew Campbell Chesnut   1820

The only "heroine" I learned of in my sixth grade American history book—a small, reddish-brown, heavily-used book with thick well-greased pages and a picture of Lewis & Clark on the front—was Betsy Ross. So when the teacher asked us to name our hero, I chose the Revolutionary War heroine, mostly because my name was also Betsy.

After Easter Chesnut's death, Abraham Chesnut's second wife, Elizabeth Chesnut, "née Blakely," took over. She was the same age as Easter's oldest child, and she produced nine more children, spaced every two to three years until she died at age 40.

Sally Chesnut   1824
William Chesnut   1826
Nancy Chesnut   1828

> Samuel Chesnut 1830
> Benjamin Chesnut 1832
> Charles Chesnut 1835
> James Edmond Chesnut 1838
> Pleasant Elly Chesnut 1840
> Margret Ann Chesnut 1842

"[Abraham Chesnut] was a real man. He had eighteen children, nine by his first wife and nine by his second." (Judge John Tully Chesnut, *St. Joseph Gazette*, Dec. 27, 1931)

Details about Betsy Ross were skimpy in my history book. Betsy was depicted as a young woman in a white Quaker cap sewing a huge American flag on her lap with George Washington standing by. Thirteen stars and thirteen stripes representing thirteen colonies—some small, some large, of different religions, some free, some slave—all sewn together.

How to express a nation?

And so it continued through the next generation, Andrew Campbell Chesnut, the last of Easter's children, married Frances Eveline Chesnut, "née Jones," who began birthing at age 19 and produced ten children, spaced one to three years apart, until she died at age 46.

> John Tully Chesnut 1839
> Abraham Thomas Chesnut 1840
> William Henry Chesnut 1843
> Mary Elizabeth Chesnut 1845
> George Flint Chesnut 1847
> Mariah Margaret Chesnut 1850
> Easter Vienna Chesnut 1853
> Francis Ann Chesnut 1856
> Samuel Andrew Chesnut 1859
> Evan Hill Chesnut 1862

"There is no slave, after all, like a wife." (Mary Chesnut's *Diary*, May 9, 1861) (no family relation)

Slavery was abolished in 1865. *Really?*

Andrew Campbell Chesnut continued with his second wife Sarah Ann Chesnut, "née Farrel," who bore three more children.

> Charles Clarence Chesnut 1869
> Lucy Saunders Chesnut 1872
> Pleasant Elly Chesnut 1875

The Catholic Church told these Irish women that producing children was the sole purpose of their lives, and the men agreed. The holy bond of marriage was indissoluble. The civil law said it was legal for men to beat their wives and force their wives to have sexual relations.

Mariah Margaret Chesnut, daughter of Andrew Campbell Chesnut and Frances Eveline Chesnut, was born in 1850, married Jacob Alphew Cox in 1872 in Buchanan County, Missouri, and produced nine children, no twins, but some spaced within 12 months of each other.

> Frederick Cox 1874
> Alvin Cox 1874
> Emma Cox 1875
> Clarence Roscoe Cox 1877
> Rosalyn Cox 1877
> William Henry Cox 1879
> Alva J. Cox 1880
> Eva Cox 1882
> Linna Cox 1884

Mariah Margaret Chesnut Cox, a tiny woman under five feet tall, had long, thick, luminous red hair, which she wound into around her head by day in a massive bun and disentangled every night with a fine-toothed comb. Her husband, Jacob Cox, knocked her down and broke her shoulder, which never healed properly. One day Jacob dragged Mariah by her hair to the woodpile and threatened to chop off her head with a hatchet. Jacob left Mariah and, without benefit of divorce, found another wife, slipped off to Oklahoma, and had four more children.

Ella Cecilia Cox, "née Hanley," was born in 1880, married William Henry Cox, son of Mariah Chesnut Cox, in 1897. She bore ten children.

Elsie May Cox 1898
Eva Cox   1900
Carl H. Cox   1902
Mildred F. Cox   1904
Cecelia M. Cox   1906
John T. Cox   1909
Edward L. Cox   1913
Mary Elizabeth Cox   1915
Norma Jane Cox   1921
Joseph Cox   1923

Ella Cox's daughter Elsie May Cox worked as a seamstress in a sweatshop in St. Joseph, Missouri making buttonholes, cuffs and collars for men's shirts. She was paid by the piece, a few pennies. In 1919, she married Paul August Rittman.

In 1920, women nationally got the right to vote. *Finally.*

Elsie May Cox Rittman taught her granddaughter Betsy how to sew by hand. Betsy learned to hem, sew on buttons, make buttonholes and to embroider with cross-stitch, backstitch, and French knot. Elsie lived to be almost 101.

A more recent, better history book provided further information: Betsy Ross, "née Griscom," was born in 1752 in Philadelphia of Quaker parents, the eighth of 17 children. After attending a Quaker school, Betsy was apprenticed to William Webster, an upholsterer. In 1773, she eloped with John Ross, a fellow apprentice. The young couple started their own upholstery shop on Chestnut Street in Philadelphia. They made mattress and chair covers, window blinds, and flags for the Pennsylvania navy.

Betsy Ross was married three times, her first two husbands casualties of the Revolutionary War. Between 1779 and 1795, she bore seven daughters.

Aucilla Ashburn   1779
Elizabeth Ashburn   1781
Clarissa Sidney Claypoole   1785
Susannah Claypoole   1786
Rachel Claypoole   1789
Jane Claypoole   1792
Harriet Claypoole   1795

Elsie May Cox Rittman played the piano by ear. She entertained her young granddaughter Betsy with "Stars and Stripes Forever," Betsy's favorite song. "By their might and by their right, it waves forever." To Elsie, the song described more than the flag, but also the struggles of her own history. It was a song from her childhood, composed in 1896 by John Philip Sousa. It was considered the "National March" and also the "Disaster March" because it was played in theaters to signal a life-threatening emergency.

Betsy Ross's grandson, William J. Canby, presented a research paper to the Historical Society of Pennsylvania in 1861. He wrote that George Washington, Commander-in-chief of the Continental Army, along with two members of the Continental Congress, Robert Morris and George Ross (Betsy's late husband's uncle), visited Betsy's upholstery shop in 1776 and commissioned an American flag. Betsy recommended five-pointed stars, not six-pointed as suggested, demonstrating how a five-pointer could be cut with one snip from a folded cloth. The story has been deemed a myth by some scholars due to lack of hard evidence and noting that the story embodies 19th century ideas about the place of women—sewing a fine seam while men bore arms. People had been too eager for Revolutionary War heroines, the scholars said.

Did historians not know that sewing the Revolutionary flag was an act of treason?

Why was it so hard to find heroines when every single soldier, every single slave was the fruit of a woman's labor, the harbinger of her death?

The Stars and Stripes evokes new meanings for each generation,
Betsy Ross's flag now flaunted as a banner for white nationalists
while distained by some African-Americans as a symbol of slavery.

How to express a nation?

> *Red the color of valor,*
> *white the color of innocence,*
> *blue the color of justice.*
> *Still?*

> *Red and white stripes*
> *like the welts on the backs of slaves,*
> *stars a brilliant vision*
> *still waiting to happen.*

George Washington Burning

Down came the statue of George Washington in Northeast Portland Oregon after protesters on Juneteenth wrapped his head in the American flag and set the flag on fire. Off with his head burn down the mission another one bites the dust. My mother is very concerned about people forgetting history oh you mean like dumping 45 tons of tea into Boston Harbor by Sons of Liberty dressed like Native Americans marching on Selma on any bloody Sunday damn Yankees taxation without representation the rocket's red glare? You can get ten years in prison for splattering the marble man with red paint who viciously enslaved one hundred African men women and children though of course I don't think of George that way after my little white girl education hero on horseback surveying the frontier leading Revolutionary warriors across the Delaware through Valley Forge becoming first president. However, I believe George would have toppled himself without the help of surly protesters because Father I cannot tell a lie while a count of 16,000 plus untruths perch on the current head it was I who chopped down the cherry tree refusing to accept beyond a second term not offhandedly making remarks about a possible third or indefinite term before even the second is secured with my little hatchet warning against bitter partisanship begging pardon for his probable many errors. Not so go Robert E. Lee and Andrew Jackson and John C. Calhoun the unrepentant pretending to stand for American values worshipped for the purpose of intimidation at lunch counters in the back of buses on the trail of tears In God We Trust righteousness rings overcome like a mighty stream Go Down Moses.

Walk a Mile in my Shoes

I wake in the morning **walking**
in plastic flip-flop **sandals**
a toddler beside me
whom I must carry
at least half the day.

A woman ahead wears **yellow**
capris which I avidly watch
till my fiery pain numbs to **ringing**
in my ears while my sandals **throb on**

even resting the dirt and rocks
of the road continue to **move**
behind my closed eyes
in my visions there is **nothing**
but feet **brown**
wrapped in **white gauze**
balm and antibiotics
                blossoming
                     blackening

if I stoop to pick up a stone
don't they know
        I have nothing
            I will be shot

a dreamer arriving
finding there is
            no dream.

Breathless Awe

Let the neck be free
feel your heels sink to earth
let your breath go out
feel it flood back in

Saguaros are bursting with water their accordion sides expanded.
Chollas capture sunlight in bright crowns of needles.

Let the neck be free
feel your heels sink to earth
exhale through your mouth
inhale through your nose

Prickly pear are outlined in halos of golden spines.
Pajaritos flit among blue oaks. Plucked leaves poke holes in my pocket.

Let your head be free
feel your heels on the earth
breathe in through your nose
the rain-washed desert air

Little burrs on the creosote hold drops of shining water.
Wait till the last minute. Wait for the worst sorrow.

Let the words be free
let the jaw go slack
feel the thick and the dark
release in whispered ahhh

As Spring Unfurls During the Pandemic

bluebirds sweep in on the southeast wind,
blackbirds hold court in the willows,
geese argue loudly for their space in the cattails,
bullfrogs sing nightly in the mud by the pond.

Spring keeps repeating and we keep rejoicing.

Yet when I appear, oh so quietly, songbirds
hear and flee, ducks hide in the reeds,
magpies scold in disdain, a muskrat
dives under water, even the geese are wary.

Truth be told, if I were not here at the pond,
if no person was ever again at the pond,
they would not miss us as if
our own mother doesn't love us.

I reflect in the still water guilt
like mud for billions of birds shot,
robbed, clearcut, poisoned, strangled.
Spring love songs are not meant for us.

The snow of isolation uncurls from the meadow,
geese are congregating two by two
in the thanksgiving of grass,
while I have no nesting instinct of my own
nor even thoughts of cleaning my house.

I gaze upon a bluebird as no bluebird can,
reveling in perch flight color
waiting winter long, longing.
All April is prayer quiet as cloud
safe as tree possible as pond breezy as hope.
On the way home I see children
have left a message on the path
surrounded by tiny white flowers
letters written in small pine cones.

Hello eve
Love
The earth

Photo by Betsy Bernfeld.

The Gulbransen

for Paul, Jr., d. 1921

It was not a Steinway
but a Gulbransen
that Paul bought her afterwards
one dollar down one dollar per week
a real stretch for their budget.
She was so attracted to the bass
notes reverberating without pedal
not trebly like a baby crying
and sometimes she would just lay
both hands on the walnut top.
She drove the Model T herself
Paul sitting next to her
the small pine box on his lap
his hands caressing the lid
her feet pounding the pedals
her fingers wringing the steering wheel
that she would refuse to ever hold again.
They would dig him up without telling her
she doesn't know where they put him
there is one photo.
A stillborn is not counted as a person
though dressed in a handmade flowing gown
meant for Baptism hand-crocheted bonnet
tied around a face battered
as he fought toward birth
high soprano accompanied by the wild deep
the photo buried in the piano bench where she sat.

Epilogue

At age four I learned the C major scale
two octaves first right hand
then left hand on the Gulbransen
and that was the end of my music education.

I never forgot even in college
right hand left hand
in the air on my lap in my bed
across the wooden table
through math English sociology philosophy.
I have taken up the piano again
long after my Grandmother played ragtime
on this same Gulbransen bench above the photo
I can't find the baby anywhere
not on the Mount Olivet Cemetery map
not even on Google
practicing the magical mathematical sequence
1 2 3 1 2 3 4 1 2 3 1 2 3 4 5
that brings calmness to the universe.

Candle
once laid on the anointing stone of Christ
once lit by the universal flame

for Paul

At one point in my life
I collected brass candlesticks
from Good Will stores
amazing how these items
could be found almost universally
in such places usually costing
fifty cents or one dollar. Once
I bought an entire box on e-bay
for two dollars. I'm sure
they are now out of style
popular during the hippie era
when kids loved opium pipes
and tinkle bells and any brass
trinkets from Southeast Asia
and cheap. Among my collection
is a small surprisingly heavy one
five inches tall and ornately carved
accommodating a thin taper
just larger than a birthday candle.
I never used it until today.

Today I inserted a thin brown
twelve-inch tall sandalwood
candle so thin and tall
that when lit it wavered
like the flame such candles sold
by the hundreds for a few cents
at an outdoor bazaar
in Jerusalem not good
for light or even décor burning
only twenty minutes but magnificent
in the end with a last flicker
and loud pop that sent

a straight line of smoke
to the ceiling which spread
and floated in aromatic
curves and waves for as long
as the candle itself had burned
sorrowing cleansing healing.

In the Forest of Unknown Trees

"it can also happen, if will and grace are joined, that as I contemplate the tree I am drawn into a relation, and the tree ceases to be an It."
Martin Buber

I am in a foreign environment
not knowing the trees by name
unsettling
I know the birds mourning doves
calling who-who
not what-what
which demands a relation
a tree as You and not It.

I stand and contemplate a tree
at the edge of a dry wash
dark green leaves drooping
like a weeping willow
clumps of trumpet flowers
off-white with purple borders
more hothouse or horticultural
than desert tree
hummingbirds chirping buzzing
oh the fragrance.

Who is this tree
I ask passersby
the white wing doves ask
who wants to know
It is I
but no one can tell me your name
must I alone translate the vision to language.

I would not choose
Chilopsis linearis
reaching higher
like Sharon Yellowfly
who translated astrophysics into Blackfoot

she called black holes birds singing
Einstein's Theory of Relativity beautiful plantings.

I stand before the beautiful planting
contemplating You
Beauty Makes Me Weep Tree.

Helianthocereus huascha rubra
Photo by Jeremy Snavely.

A Sip from the Claret Cup

At first I thought the cactus was a claret cup
hedgehog, an inglorious name barely hinting
at the brilliant red blooms that showed up
on Mother's Day in the brick planter box
that graced the house from front door
to street built 60 years ago by my father.

After a lifetime of white cars and beige
my father bought my mother a red Toyota,
easy to watch her comings and goings
from his hospital window.

In the beginning the planter box was filled
with good soil and steer manure and boomed
with African daisies. In passing years
enthusiasm for gardening waned and the box
stayed empty except for a purple lantana
that jumped over from the side yard.

That first Valentine's Day without him
a red rose appeared under her windshield wiper.

Propagated by seed, seven years to bloom,
said the encyclopedia, so the cactus
must have arrived near my father's death
perhaps on the wings of a mourning dove.

Prefers strong bright light, volcanic gravels.
Avoid any hint of wet soil.

The year following the first stunning bloom
as my mother drove home in the red Toyota,
she maneuvered to the left side of the street
to check the mailbox and noticed the red buds
on the cactus getting ready to open this time
in March a few days before her birthday.

*Red so bold against the bleak colors
of the desert.*

No Arizona native cactus blooms more
than once a year, I'm told, one gorgeous day
of flamboyant flowers then closing at night
and dying. But this cactus bore blossoms
again in April on my father's birthday a mystery
but still it could be scientifically explained,
I'm sure, without miracle or metaphor.

Red for suffering, fire atop a needled arm.

The claret cup is fertilized by hummingbirds,
I've learned. To sip from the nectar chamber
they must plunge their entire heads into the red
petals coating bill, face and neck in pollen
diving deep into reality to its core the divine.

*Red like a siren song, seductive, deceptive,
dangerous, irresistible.*

The horticulturist I consulted supplied
a long Latin name (curious that both botany
and the Holy Romans share the dead
language). *Helianthocereus huascha rubra*,
South American hybrid, nickname "Glorious."

In this year of no rain, more than 100 days
of drought, the cactus bloomed in April, May,
June, July. My mother felt in her bones
as they became weaker that he was calling her,
now more adamantly, more urgently
to join him in a cup of red wine.

At Rachel's Well

Action precedes prayer
in ceremony just this one time
said the rabbi.

Thus the Mikveh began
with immersion
in Rachel's Well
all the way under water
eyes open fingers and toes
spread apart hair floating
in long loose curls wedding
ring removed even nail
polish rubbed off all breath
expelled from her lungs.

Outside in the August heat
maple seeds flew off the trees
like whirligigs like angel
wings like butterfly
dancers bronze and brown
and blond delicately veined
landing upright in the soil
just waiting to be pushed
into earth by paw or snow.

The well holds living water
from a river or natural spring
or just plain rain but
never carried in a bucket
diverted directly from
roof to its own cistern then
allowed to kiss through
a tiny drain to the larger
pool for ritual.

Outside in the garden cool
hummingbirds buzzed

in constant hum like
bumblebees like katydids
on a desert eve one hovering
several seconds near my face
its proud neck white and purple
green whirligig wings
perhaps preparing for
its own solitary migration.

In the month of Elul
the season of preparation
for High Holy Days the word
itself a Hebrew acronym
I am my beloved's
and my beloved is mine.
Three immersions
for conversion
for completeness
for purity
then finally prayers.

A Hebrew Lamentation

for Eve

Ninety-nine years old
God still sent a child,
filled her sky with stars
after all those years.
Hear the angels well,
they have come to tell
of the pending birth.
Make the bed
find the clothes
stoke the fire
draw the bath
ninety-nine years old
and Sarah laughed.

Rachel craved a child,
Leah had ten sons,
didn't matter that
she was Jake's first love,
so she sighed and wept
and she begged God's help.
After years of hope
after days of pain
make the bed
find the clothes
stoke the fire
draw the bath
Baby Joe was born
and Rachel laughed.

Hannah lay face down
on the temple stone
like a sot she moaned,
cried and screamed her prayer.
Rabbi thought her drunk
tried to throw her out

but she clung to the
rock and she was saved.
Make the bed
find the clothes
stoke the fire
draw the bath
Hannah got her child
curly locks and all
Baby Sam was born
and Hannah laughed.

Nazareth was shocked
'Lizabeth was fat.
Why is that, poor soul,
at your age and all?
Zechariah was
struck dumb at his job
inside the Holies.
How could wife so long
barren, oh my God,
at last conceive? What's
the deal, who's to blame,
praise Elijah.
Make the bed
find the clothes
stoke the fire
draw the bath
Old Zech spoke again,
his name is John.

Mary sat in prayer
for a son to come
to the world—not her
for the good of all.
Not once did she think
it would be her task
to bring the Son of God
to the world at last.
Her son was to die

a sword was to pierce
both him and her.
Make the bed
find the clothes
stoke the fire
draw the bath
the Christ was born
to the world
with Mary's yes.

In early dawn of
the world's first morning
it was Eve who longed
for her Adam's child
but pride had locked her
from the garden where
God had walked in the
evening light. But save
me still, so desolate,
she cried in labor
from the plain. And God
came back to rescue
her amid her harsh
and searing pain just
take my hand, you will
have three sons or more.
Make the bed
find the clothes
stoke the fire
draw the bath
God is near
a child is born.

Hebrew elegiac poetry has a characteristic limping, halting rhythm called kinah. It is said to conform to the natural pattern of grief—abrupt, mournful, unembellished—flowing directly from the heart. It was chanted or sung by professional mourners. Lines typically consist of an unbalanced five beats, the first three strong, followed by a half-rest, then a quiet, two-beat, echoing rhythm.

Zero Percent Contained

Wildfire blew up in Cliff Creek
caused by lightning strike on beetle-killed pines
and dry sagebrush jumping immediately
to 6,000 acres marching straight north into
the Gros Ventre Wilderness but not far from
my tiny log cabin in the forest near Bondurant.
Residents in Granite Creek campground
were forced to flee house on fire hair on fire.
A note on my cabin door said prepare
to evacuate upon a moment's notice.
The next day's incident report
showed 17,000 acres involved
551 firefighters dispatched
fixed wing and helicopters in the air
zero percent chance of rain
fire zero percent contained.

I remember in seventh grade science
we had to rank a list of 15 items
most important to take with us
from our crashed spacecraft to the mother ship
if stranded on the moon. The correct answer
was number one oxygen not relevant here.
Next of course was water a distant third food.
Nothing about a box of poetry. Rope and parachute silk
got surprisingly high ratings while guns and matches
surprisingly low. In retrospect
oxygen might have been helpful and
poems tell much more than photos.

First thing I put three gallon jugs of water
that once held cranberry juice in the back of the car
then a small box of cans—tuna beef stew corn
pears string beans—with a can opener
tent sleeping bag and poems.
What would be the use of saving
my old raggedy clothes from the flames?

I bought two new tee-shirts and a pair of jeans.
I did take a gun my only possession worth much
a double barreled 20-gauge Belgian Browning Diana
and the silver bracelet with turquoise inlays
my mother gave me all tucked neatly in the car
car keys on the kitchen table
car parked by the front door but
where can I go so imprisoned in this life
sun glaring red through smoke.

Fire now 27,868 acres new weather pattern
new wind direction gusts to forty understory
dry and receptive long term analysis
50 percent contained by September 30.
The order came via my cell phone
a blasting emergency signal in the middle of the night
evacuate immediately keys on the kitchen table
car parked by the front door smoke
slinking in through chinks in the chinking
and open corners where mice have excavated
where can I go so imprisoned but
my soul zero percent contained
pouring out like white vapor
back through the chinks in the chinking
and open corners created by mice
house on fire hair on fire flush
of wildflowers predicted for spring.

Mother in the City of God

Morning after morning the sunrise
erupts in brilliant vermillion
horizon to horizon
after a night of sirens
helicopters circling with searchlights
motorcycles racing through the gears
down main street
while Mother sleeps.

Day after day the city sizzles
in record-breaking temperature
crime plunder drug traffic
stacks of rusting cars Mother
in pain now with a broken tooth
compressed vertebra
wind etching alkaline tears down the sides
of bleached out buildings.

Driving north there are the mountains
driving south there are the mountains
east and west blue mountains
pink in sunrise and sunset
like the bliss of her arrival
the birth of her five daughters
paradise withering like blistered dreams
grass turning yellow never green.

Once again before the terrible night
the sky explodes in orange
magenta gold green rose purple
like the chant of a psalm at vespers
but after vespers the nuns in black
fade back into the cloister
Mother into her pink chair by the TV
a final burst of color.

Sacred Heart Chapel
Grand Teton National Park
Photo by Betsy Bernfeld.

Walking through the Mercy Door at Sacred Heart Chapel on Summer Solstice under Strawberry Moon

There could not be any more light than this light,
a cloudless day on the longest day of the year,
then the full moon at sundown climbing high and amber
throughout the night when Algonquins picked wild strawberries.

In the dark chapel the only light filtered in through
a round stained glass pane in the center of the north wall,
that entering light first bouncing off the high snowbound peaks,
the tempestuous blue lake, and the acre of arrowleaf
balsamroot blooming from the shore to the church,
funneling in through the circle of clouded white glass,
a red heart in its center, shaped like a strawberry
surrounded by thorns, all light concentrated
on a single torn heart.

Wrath came in with me through the mercy door,
sat in the pew with me, my eyes pushing back
through the sacred window, through the heart
into the bright light with peaceful light piercing
my own heart, like Algonquins bequeathing Thanksgiving
rewarded with bloodshed and betrayal,
the mercy door slamming,
opening and slamming.

Acknowledgments

Grateful acknowledgment is made to the editors of the following journals, chapbook and exhibit where these poems first appeared:

"The Woman and the Coyote" and "A Sip from the Claret Cup" in *Southwestern American Literature.*

"Zero Percent Contained" in *Manifest West—Transitions & Transformations.*

"Cathedral" and "If I Were Going to Build a House" in *Eve,* published by Finishing Line Press.

"Trespass at 820 East Grant" in the "Poetry Apothecary" Exhibit at the Jackson Hole Center for the Arts.

Grateful acknowledgment is made to the artists who allowed the use of their works in this chapbook:

Cover & Interior Art: "The Mothers: *Las Madres Project. No Mas Lágrimas*" created by Valarie Lee James with Antonia Gallegos, Deborah McCullough and Cesar Lopez., 2005. The sculptures are part of a public art installation in Tucson, Arizona. The statues were made from desert plants and strips of the clothing left along the way by migrants, each *Madre* representing 1,000 who have died crossing the Sonoran Desert.

Alamo Wash Mosaic: "Marble Waters" created by Robin Riley, 2008. Part of a Public Arts Project sponsored by Pima County and the Tucson Pima County Arts Council.

Many thanks to Alicia Whissel for her brilliant assistance with social media, to "the nephews" Jeremy and Jon for photography help, and to my husband Joe for his constant support.

Work on this volume has been supported in part by an award from the Wyoming Arts Council through funding from the National Endowment for the Arts.

About the Author

Originally from Tucson, Arizona, **Betsy Orient Bernfeld** is a writer, librarian and lawyer in Jackson Hole, Wyoming. She has received awards for her journalism and fiction, and three of her short plays have been produced by Wyoming community theater companies. Her anthology of historical Wyoming poetry, *Sagebrush Classics: Pure Wyoming Stuph*, was published by Media Publishing in Kansas City, MO, and her own poems have recently appeared in *Black Hills Literary Journal; High Desert Journal; Manifest West; Third Wednesday; Crosswinds Poetry Journal; Southwestern American Literature; Blood, Water, Wind, and Stone: An Anthology of Wyoming Writers*; and three WyoPoets chapbooks: *Labyrinth, This Box for Dreams,* and *Watershed*.

Betsy's poetry chapbook, entitled *Eve*, was released by Finishing Line Press in 2018. She is winner of the Wyoming Arts Council's 2020 Creative Writing Fellowship for Poetry. In her latest collection, *The Cathedral Is Burning*, Betsy's poetry dances between desert and mountains, cathedral and home in a lamentation for the loss of Mothers, Grandmothers and Mother Earth.

www.ingramcontent.com/pod-product-compliance
Lightning Source LLC
Chambersburg PA
CBHW042145160426
43201CB00022B/2411